A GOOD HELPING

RECIPES FROM CANTERBURY AND DISTRICT SAMARITANS

SAMARITANS
Canterbury & District

First edition published 2022

Published under licence by Canterbury and District Samaritans, 32 Northgate Canterbury CT1 1BL
https://www.samaritans.org/branches/canterbury/

ISBN: 978-1-3999-3708-5

In aid of

SAMARITANS
Canterbury & District

Canterbury and District Samaritans is a charity registered in England and Wales
(1166874)

A GOOD HELPING

Recipes From Canterbury and District Samaritans

SAMARITANS
Canterbury & District

CONTENTS

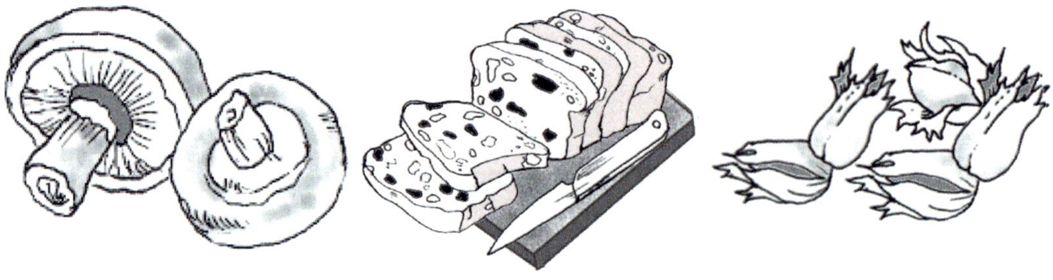

INTRODUCTION

When training to become a Samaritans volunteer, I remember being shown an image of how someone might look before they call Samaritans. This person looked like they were at crisis point and didn't know which way to turn. Samaritans are there to listen and can help people find their own way through whatever is troubling them. Listening could save someone's life.

Much like a seed reaching through the dirt toward light, positive growth can occur from within. With support and love, seeds can not only grow, but flourish too. Nature offers so much positivity, that just spending quality time with nature has been proven to have an encouraging effect on mood, both from the outside and from within.

High-fibre foods such as fruit, vegetables and whole grains are recommended as part of a diverse diet. Just as important are the foods we use to nurture ourselves, food which evokes precious memories, dishes we cook for loved ones and simple food we use to comfort ourselves when things are tough.

We hope that the range of recipes here can help you work towards improved inner health, and even more so if you've been able to nurture and grow any of the ingredients yourself. As you look through these recipes, please think about how caring for yourself and each other by eating healthily is a life priority we should all be aiming for. We are like seeds and having the right environment within, and all around us will create space for us to grow in beautiful and surprising ways. The right environment includes the right people, who are like seeds too, but seeds you feel love and friendship towards. And that feeling in your gut? That could be the delicate excitement of having a crowded table, full of positive growth.

Tom 308, Director,
Canterbury and District Samaritans

These recipes were gathered from volunteers at Canterbury and District Samaritans and our community. The dishes are what we like to eat and are special to us.

Some of the recipes remind us of people and places dear to us and important parts of our lives. Some are our comfort eats; others provide continuity and the "glue" which keeps families and communities together. Recipes are handed on and enjoyment shared.

Not all of our volunteers wanted to be acknowledged in their recipes so there are more people involved in the making of this book than we have been able to list. Samaritans volunteers give their time generously and without recognition and the branch as a whole has contributed to this project to raise money to keep the vital work we do running twenty-four hours a day.

All of the profits from the book will be used to support callers at our Canterbury and District Branch.

BREAKFAST AND BRUNCH

GRAHAM'S PORRIDGE

If the summers of my childhood seemed longer and hotter than they do now, then the winters were most definitely colder and almost never ending, seeming to stretch from late October through to the end of March and even on into April. Proper winters - with snowdrifts and power cuts and ice on the inside of the windows of our non-centrally heated house.

Ingredients per person:

- 50g rolled oats
- water as required
- milk as required

Extras:

Whatever makes it feel good for you.

Equipment required:

- heavy bottomed saucepan
- spurtle*
- patience

Whether heading off to school or, if the snow was too deep or the temperature too low for it to open, to the nearby slopes for sledging fun and snowball fights, a bowl of Mum's home-made porridge was guaranteed to warm me through to face the day. If chicken soup is Jewish penicillin, then Mum's porridge was Scottish winter sunshine in a bowl.

These days, even in the milder, drier winters of Kent, a great steaming bowl made the way she used to make it, hot enough to take the skin off the roof of your mouth, is enough to give me that feeling of inner warmth and contentment I remember from those days. Every Scottish mum had her own recipe; this is mine.

Method

Place the oats in the saucepan and cover with just enough water to leave a little puddle on the top when gently stirred. If you're leaving them to soak overnight then add a little more, cover and place in the fridge.

Leave to soak for at least 20 minutes. (If you're in a hurry pour boiling water over the oats, stir and move on to the next stage).

Place on the heat source and add approximately the same amount of milk as water used in stage 1.

Stir continuously with your spurtle* - always clockwise, never Widdershins or you'll bring the Devil and his bad luck to your door. (Thanks for the nightmares, Mum!).

When the porridge starts to bubble, reduce the heat and continue to stir, adding water or milk until you have the consistency you prefer. I add salt at this point but that's my preference and you may prefer it sweet.

Taste the mix after about 5 minutes. At this point the oats should still be slightly crunchy. If you prefer them softer, stir for a little longer.

When the consistency is to your liking, pour into a warmed bowl. This is where you can get creative and make your own favourite feel-good breakfast porridge. As I said earlier, I prefer mine with salt but some prefer sweet. My family is split about fifty-fifty on this and it probably generates more "discussion" than the Independence Referendum ever did.

You can add a dollop of cream or yoghurt if you want. Or sugar, honey, maple syrup, berries, nuts, banana, coconut flakes, grated nutmeg - whatever makes you feel good.
I've even been known to stir in a few drops of a fine Island Malt Whisky to make it a proper feel-good start to the day.

'Ith do shàth! Eat your fill! (Pronounced EEch doh HAH)

*Narrow bladed wooden spoon/stick for stirring porridge ... Anti-clockwise

JASMINE'S PECAN AND MAPLE GRANOLA

I lived in Canada for a couple of years, and while I was there, I discovered a cousin that I never knew I had. This is my take on a granola that was introduced to me in Vancouver when returning there for my cousin's daughter's wedding in 2019. The bride-to-be brought over some over to us when we landed from the UK, and it was the toastiest and tastiest welcome we could have asked for! While I've adapted it, each time I make a batch, I think of Katherine, so it's a reminder of distant family that I no longer get to see on a regular basis. This recipe has been converted into UK measuring cups so uses volume but approximate weights have been given.

Preparation time: 10 mins

Cooking time: approx. 40 mins

Ingredients:

- 3 cups (270g) jumbo rolled oats
- 1 cup (120g) pumpkin seeds
- 1 cup (120g) sunflower seeds
- 1 cup (95g) raw coconut chips
- 1 1/2 cups (150g) roughly chopped pecans
- 3/4 cup of maple syrup (250g) (pure) - I often adjust this down to reduce the sweetness
- 1/2 cup (110g) extra virgin olive oil
- 1/2 cup (100g) soft brown sugar
- 1 pinch of salt.

Method

Heat the oven to 140 degrees (gas mark 2)

Mix all the ingredients together in a large bowl, ensuring that the oil and syrup are well-mixed into the dry ingredients.

Spread the mixture in an even layer on a rimmed baking sheet.

Put in the oven and bake, turning the granola over every 10 minutes until toasted. (Approx 40 minutes depending on your oven)

Remove from the oven and let cool completely before serving or storing in an airtight container for up to one month.

DANI'S VEGAN SCRAMBLED TOFU

This makes a substantial breakfast or brunch.

Method

Chop the spring onions, peppers and garlic and fry these in non-stick pan for 2 minutes.

Drain the tofu and add to the pan, stirring frequently. (I use a small handheld whisk to stir as it breaks the tofu up into small pieces.)

Add the remaining ground ingredients while continuing to stir. Tofu can be very bland; whilst the ground ingredients are optional, it does give it a lovely colour and a good flavour.

Serve with toast and whatever else takes your fancy!

Ingredients:

- 60g silken tofu
- 2 tbsp olive oil
- 4 spring onions
- ½ red pepper
- ½ orange pepper
- 1 clove garlic
- ½ tsp ground turmeric optional
- ½ tsp ground cumin
- ½ tsp ground coriander

TOM'S VEGAN SPINACH AND KALE SMOOTHIE

An ultra-healthy pick-you-up for the start of the day.

Method

All ingredients popped in a blender and blitzed for one minute.

Serve straight away.

Preparation Time: 5 minutes
Makes: 2 (half pint glasses)
Ingredients:

- 1 apple, core removed, cut up, peel left on
- 1 banana
- handful of washed spinach
- handful of washed kale
- half a teaspoon of green spirulina powder
- half a teaspoon of ginger
- teaspoon of cinnamon
- two cubes of ice
- 500ml of Oat milk

AVO-CUDDLE

Two recipes from the Coffee Corner Canterbury. This new café is an ideal place to treat yourself to a comfortable, leisurely brunch.

Ingredients for 2

- 2 ripe avocado
- 4 slices of sour-dough bread
- 4 eggs
- large handful of baby leaf salad
- 2 tablespoons of balsamic glaze
- teaspoon lime
- teaspoon of vinegar

Method

In a medium saucepan bring ½ litre of water and the vinegar to the boil. Gently swirl the water with a large spoon and then once the water is turning crack your eggs into the water.

Keep the water simmering for 3-6 mins until your poached eggs are cooked to your liking (3 mins soft – 6 mins medium hard). Yo,u can also use other methods to poach your eggs, such as a poacher or microwave.

Whilst the eggs are poaching, cut the avocados in half, remove the stone, and scrape the flesh into a medium sized bowl and mash together with a good pinch of salt and pepper and a teaspoon of lime.

Spread the avocado mixture on the 4 sourdough slices.

Once the eggs are cooked, remove them from the water and make sure the eggs are drained well. You can place them on a paper towel to remove excess water.

Place the eggs on top of the avocado mix.

In a medium bowl place the baby leaf salad and add the balsamic glaze and give it a good mix up. Split the salad in half and serve on the side or in a separate bowl.

Coffee Corner
51 St. Dunstan's Street
Canterbury CT2 8BS.

EGGS BENEDICT

Another recipe from the Coffee Corner Canterbury. You can buy a jar of Hollandaise sauce for this recipe if you like. It will be nearly, if not quite, as good.

Ingredients for 2

- 150g smoked salmon or ham
- 2 English muffins cut in half
- 4 eggs
- 25g chives
- 1 teaspoon of vinegar

Hollandaise sauce:

- 125g butter
- 2 egg yolks
- ½ teaspoon of white wine vinegar
- squeeze lemon juice

Method

Hollandaise sauce:

Melt the butter in a small saucepan.
Put on another saucepan of simmering water.
Put the yolks, vinegar and a pinch of salt in a heat proof bowl that will fit over the saucepan of water.
Whisk the yolk mixture for a few minutes, then place it over the simmering water and continue to whisk until thick and pale. (3-5 mins)
Once you have the thick consistency you then need to take it off the heat and slowly dribble the melted butter into the mixture whilst continuously whisking.
If it is a little too thick add a splash of water. Keep the mixture warm.

Eggs Benedict:

In a medium saucepan bring ½ litre of water and the vinegar to the boil. Gently swirl the water with a large spoon and then once the water is turning, crack your eggs into the water. Keep the water simmering for 3 - 6 mins until your poached eggs are cooked to your liking (3 mins soft – 6 mins medium hard). You can also use other methods to poach your eggs, such as a poacher or microwave.

Whilst the eggs are cooking, place the salmon or ham on top of each muffin half.
Once the eggs are cooked, remove them from the water and make sure the eggs are drained well. You can place them on a paper towel to remove excess water.
Place the eggs on top of the ham or salmon.
Pour or spoon the warm hollandaise over the eggs.
You can toast and butter the muffins if you prefer.

JAN'S OTHER HALF'S HOLIDAY BREAKFAST

Whilst staying at Gwesty Cymru on Aberystwyth seafront, the chef's way of serving kippers was so delicious that Jan's other half had it two mornings running.

Ingredients:

- 1 slice of sourdough bread
- 1 smoked Manx kipper
- a sprig of cherry tomatoes
- a good handful of spinach
- salt, pepper, rapeseed & olive oil
- parsley oil *

Method

Toast the bread, grill the kipper for 4 / 5 minutes.

Season and roast the tomatoes in olive oil for 10 minutes.

Wilt the spinach in a knob of butter. In another pan froth some butter to make brown butter.

Top toast with spinach, then with the kipper and tomatoes.

Pour over the brown butter.

To make it even more delicious drizzle over some parsley oil* and chopped parsley.

(*This is made by the chef in Gwesty Cymru by blending equal amounts of parsley with rapeseed oil. Sieve into a metal bowl. Freeze for 3 hours, pour off the oil to use.)

GWESTY CYMRU
HOTEL & RESTAURANT

Gwesty Cymru,
19 Marine Terrace, Aberystwyth, Ceredigion. SY23 2AZ
info@gwestycymru.co.uk

STARTERS

PHOEBE'S SWEET POTATO AND CHORIZO SOUP WITH HOME-MADE CROUTONS

This recipe is a hearty, warming soup which makes a satisfying light lunch. It makes about 6 litres of soup, serves about 20 good portions. Adjust accordingly! The soup will keep for 2 / 3 days stored cold. Heat what you need each time.

Ingredients:

- ½ bag of potatoes (approx. 1Kg)
- 8 medium sweet potatoes
- 4 or 5 vegetable or chicken stock cubes
- 3 medium red onions
- 1 whole, spiced chorizo sausage
- 1 tsp paprika / 1 tsp garlic granules
- salt and pepper to taste

Method

Wash and dice all of the potatoes.

Dice the red onion.

Dice the chorizo sausage (the skin can be discarded).

Add all of the ingredients to a large pan with enough water to cover. Grate the stock cubes into the pan. Bring everything to the boil for about 10 minutes, then reduce the heat and simmer for about an hour.

Check that everything is cooked, then blitz with a hand blender until semi-smooth. Check the taste and add another stock cube or paprika if needed. Serve hot with home-made croutons.

Home-Made Croutons

Dice some bread into cubes and place in a bowl. Drizzle with some vegetable oil, mixed herbs and garlic granules and toss together.
Line a baking tray with parchment and spread the croutons evenly over it.
Bake at 180º C, gas mark 4 for 10 / 15 minutes.

Leave to cool and store in an airtight container.

Add the croutons to the soup, and add a little double cream as a decoration.

A VOLUNTEER'S TASTE OF ITALY

This recipe is a favourite of all the family and we often have this at Christmas as it is refreshing and light before the turkey roast

Ingredients: serves 2

- 1 large beef tomato
- 4 slices of Parma ham
- 10 fresh basil leaves
- drizzle of balsamic glaze
- drizzle of olive oil
- grind of salt and pepper
- ball of mozzarella

Method

Slice the mozzarella ball into 6 slices.

Slice the Beef tomato into 6 even pieces. You can discard the ends, but we use them so as not to waste anything.

On a small plate overlap the slices of Tomato and Mozzarella, so you have 3 of each alternately placed across your plate.

Then scrunch your Parma Ham and place them under the tomato and mozzarella strip.
You can place the ingredients however you fancy, but this works for us.

Once everything is in place take 5 basil leaves and place them around the plate.

Give everything a grind of salt and pepper to taste.

Finally drizzle the balsamic glaze and olive oil over the top, again this can be quite creative if you feel up to it.

WILD GARLIC SOUP

Wild garlic starts to appear in woodland in late February/early March. I love this soup as it is as simple to make as it is delicious, the added bonus being that it's super-nutritious too. I really like this soup with the addition of a little crème fraiche in each bowl and a good drizzle of wild garlic oil.

Ingredients:

-2 large leeks, halved and washed
-2 cloves of garlic, peeled and halved
-50g butter
-2 large floury potatoes
-4 big handfuls of wild garlic leaves, washed
-1 pint of milk

Method

Heat your oven to 200c and bake the potatoes until cooked through, 50 minutes or so. Bring a large pan of salted water to the boil.

Meanwhile cut away the dark green part of the leeks, save this for stock. Finely slice the remaining white and pale green part of the leek and stew in the butter along with the garlic and a large pinch of salt, continue slowly cooking in this fashion until all is soft.

Meanwhile, blanch the wild garlic. Once the large pan of water is at a rolling boil add the wild garlic and cook for a minute and a half.

Drain the wild garlic and refresh under cold water or even better in a bowl of iced water. Once cold, drain the wild garlic again and squeeze out the excess water with your hands. Transfer to a chopping board and coarsely chop.
Bring the milk to a simmer then switch off the heat.

Once the potatoes have cooked allow to cool enough for you to cut them in half. Scoop out their soft flesh and add to the pan of soft sweet leeks. Turn up the heat under the leeks and add the wild garlic and the milk.

Have ready a liquidizer. Once the soup comes to a simmer, switch off the heat and start blending the soup in batches. Don't overfill!
Allow the soup to blend for three minutes or so, then pass through a sieve into a clean pan (or container if storing for later use), press on the solids with the back of a ladle to extract maximum goodness.
Now taste, adjust the seasoning if necessary and reheat until hot, but not boiling. Serve in warmed bowls

David Hart, Folkestone Wine Company
https://folkestonewine.com/

FESTIVE FISH PÂTÉ

This is a decorative and flavoursome start to the meal. There is no cooking involved, which must be good.

Preparation time: 30 mins + freezing / chilling
Cooking time: Nil
Serves: 10 – 12

Ingredients:

- ½ red pepper
- 1 small tin anchovy fillet
- 8 stuffed olives
- 3 x 120g tins sardines in tomato sauce
- 230g cream or curd cheese
- 115g fresh breadcrumbs
- rind of 1 lemon
- 2 hard-boiled eggs
- 85g butter
- 2 tbsp chopped parsley

To serve:
toast and salad garnish

Method

Hard boil the 2 eggs.

Line a 2 lb loaf tin both ways to make the pate easier to remove.

Cut the pepper into strips and place alternately with the anchovies along the base of the tin. (The anchovies can be rinsed to remove some of the salt if you wish.)
Cut the olives in half and place face-side down at intervals.

Soften the butter and place in a large bowl with the breadcrumbs, cheese and lemon rind cut into small strips.

Mash everything together.
Drain the sardines and mash with a fork. If the mixture feels dry add some of the tomato juice from the fish until it is moist.
Chop the hard-boiled eggs and fold in.

Push the mixture down firmly on top of the anchovies and peppers in the tin.

It is best to freeze the pate in the tin. It can be chilled overnight but this will make a softer pate. Remove the pate from the tin using the cling film and defrost in the fridge for about 3 hours.

It will make a better-looking dish if it is sliced while frozen.

JAMES'S SIMPLE STUFFED TOMATOES

This is a Belgian classic starter. It has a retro, nostalgic feel for us, reminiscent of time spent living in Brussels. The quality of the ingredients is key for this recipe. Seek out very ripe tomatoes, beefsteak for choice. In Belgium this is often made with small, brown shrimps but any good quality shrimp or prawn will do.

Ingredients:

- 1 large, ripe tomato per person
- 25g brown shrimps or prawns per person
- mayonnaise
- lemon juice
- black pepper

Method

Cut the top off the tomato to make a lid. You may need to take a small slice of the bottom to make the tomatoes stand up firmly.

Scoop the core and seeds from the tomatoes and use for something else. Let any juice drain off.

Mix the prawns or shrimps with a squeeze of lemon and enough mayonnaise to cover them generously.

Spoon the filling into the tomato shells and put the "lid" on top.

Serve with good bread and butter.

ONION SOUP

This is a very economical and reliable recipe for a quick meal.

Method

Slice the onion finely and fry gently in the olive oil until golden and soft. This will take about 20 minutes.

When they are done, sprinkle them with a little sugar.

Add the water and stock cube and boil for 20 mins.

Turn the heat down to a gentle simmer and add the white wine. Simmer for another 10 mins.

Divide the soup between 4 bowls, float a piece of toast in each bowl and divide the cheese between the toasts. Put the bowls under a hot grill until the cheese is melted and crispy.

If you can use a good beef stock this soup will be even better.

Ingredients:

- 2 or 3 medium onions
- 1 litre water
- wineglass of white wine
- I stock cube
- approx. 30ml olive oil
- 100g grated Gruyere cheese
- 4 rounds toasted French bread
- a little sugar
- salt and pepper

TAPENADE

You can do so much with tapenade. Use it as a dip, toss it through pasta, spread it on toast. This recipe suggests you serve it with fresh bread but you can use it as a dip for sliced vegetables. A recipe for all occasions!

Preparation time: 20 mins

Ingredients: serves 6

- -175g pitted black olives
- 50g anchovy fillets
- 30ml (2tsp) capers
- 120 ml olive oil
- zest of 1 lemon
- ground black pepper

Method

Finely chop the olives, anchovies and capers and beat together with the oil and lemon rind.

You could use a blender or food processor. This will make a finer tapenade, perhaps not as authentic as the rougher texture created when it is chopped by hand.

Season with pepper and add a little more olive oil if it seems too dry.

Transfer to a small to medium deep dish and serve with wholemeal bread. Even better, serve with some of the olive bread you will find in the baking section.

MAINS

PETER'S FISH WITH LEEKS AND MUSHROOMS IN CREAM

This reminds me of a visit to our very good friends who moved away from Canterbury many years ago. We visited them a few years back (pre-lockdown) and it was great meeting up and catching up with news of all our kids politics and general stuff. Our friends served us this delicious meal accompanied with a bottle of chilled white wine. It's such a tasty dish and can be as low calorie as you want or stick with the lip-smackingly scrumptious full fat version. Admittedly, I didn't ask for an actual recipe, but we talked enough about it for me to able to recreate it back home.
Portion size? This is really up to you. I am writing this right now as a dish for two people with really good appetites. Keep in mind, I tend to overestimate and reheat in the microwave for lunch the next day – assuming I can resist the temptation to polish it all off in one go – which is rare.

Ingredients:

- 300ml fresh sour cream or double cream or crème fraiche or Greek yoghurt, swap out for low fat if you want.
- 1 large baking potato
- 250g button mushrooms
- 1 large leek
- 25g butter
- 300g of firm-fleshed fish of your choice.
- salt and pepper to season
- 25g grated cheddar cheese to sprinkle on a few minutes before serving.
- a sprinkling of freshly grated nutmeg to go on at the very end.

Method

Wash your potato (with skins on) and cut into bite-size pieces

Add the potatoes to a pan of water and bring to boil, once boiling reduce the heat and simmer for approximately 6 mins or until tender. Be careful not to over cook as the potato will disintegrate. Once cooked drain and place to one side. (or steam your potatoes if you prefer)

While the potato is cooking split and remove the outer leaves of the leek and wash thoroughly removing any dirt.

Cut your leeks into rings of 1.5cm, you may need to wash again as leeks tend to hide dirt in them

Clean the button mushrooms and leave whole; if large they can be halved/quartered or sliced

Heat a large wide based non-stick pan (that has a lid) and add the butter. Once melted add the mushrooms and cook until soft and slightly brown.

Once the mushrooms are turning brown add the leek rounds and a pinch of salt and a good grind of pepper and give it a good mix up. Put the lid on and cook for about 10 minutes. Give it a swirl with the lid on to avoid it catching.

While the leeks and mushrooms are cooking, cut your chosen fish into bite-size chunks and set to one side. Once the leeks and mushrooms are cooked add your potato chunks to the pan and mix carefully together.

Then add your fish on top of the mixture and put the lid back on and cook for about 10-15 minutes or until the fish is pearlescent, tender and flaky.

The mushrooms and leeks create a nice amount of liquor but feel free to add a bit of butter if it's looking too dry. (If you keep the lid on, you probably won't need to add anything extra.) Don't be tempted to stir as you don't want the potatoes and fish to break up - just check to see when the fish is done.

Once cooked take the pan off the heat. Pour over the cream (or whatever you have chosen), but note that cream or yoghurt tend to curdle if added to a boiling sauce.

Lastly add the nutmeg and grated cheese and put the lid back on to help the cheese melt.

Finally, take the pan to table and serve. Doesn't need any sides - enjoy!

MUSHROOM AND CRISPY BACON RISOTTO

This is one of my 'desert island dishes'. If stuck on a desert island with my choice of limited ingredients, what 3 meals would I live on? Risotto is at the top of the list.

Ingredients for 2:

- 1 onion
- tbsp of finely chopped parsley
- 40g grated parmesan cheese
- 150g chestnut mushrooms
- 700ml of vegetable or chicken stock
- 1 crushed garlic clove
- 100g smoked bacon lardons
- 50ml white wine
- 160g Arborio rice
- pepper

Method

Heat a large deep-frying pan with a drizzle of vegetable oil. Once hot add the lardons and cook until crispy.

While the lardons are cooking, keeping an eye on them, finely chop the onion, and roughly chop the mushrooms.

Once the lardons are crispy, put them into a bowl and keep to one side as you will add these at the end of cooking to keep them crispy.

Add to the pan the onions, mushrooms, crushed garlic, and a good grind of black pepper and cook for 3-4 mins.

Once the onions have started to soften add the Arborio rice and wine and cook for 2 minutes to burn off the alcohol

Then gradually add the stock a little at a time and wait for the stock to be absorbed before adding more. Continue to do this until all of the stock has been absorbed and the rice is cooked.

Then add half the parmesan cheese and parsley and mix through the risotto.

Serve in warm bowls and garnish with the remaining parmesan cheese and parsley. It is delicious on its own or with warm garlic bread.

JAN'S ROAST VEGETABLE SUPPER

I made this together with my daughter who was recovering from an illness and we enjoyed feeling rather full afterwards.

Ingredients: serves 4

- 1 sweet potato
- 1 butternut squash
- 2 large red onions
- 2 large carrots
- 2 medium courgettes
- or whatever other veg you have lurking in your fridge!
- several cloves of garlic
- a block of feta cheese
- a cupful of defrosted frozen peas
- a handful of fresh coriander
- cayenne pepper, mustard seeds, salt
- olive oil
- 150g of cooked pearl barley.
- tbsp runny honey

Method

In a large roasting tin add a liberal amount of olive oil and some crushed garlic cloves.

Put it in a hot oven whilst you chop all the veg into 1 inch cubes.

Add the veg to a large roasting tin (except the courgettes) plus spices to season.

Roast for about 20 to 25 minutes, add the courgettes and roast for another 20 minutes. Drizzle a tablespoon of runny honey over the veg.

Meanwhile cook the pearl barley until just done, then strain and rinse with boiling water.

Take the tin out of the oven stir in the barley and top with the chopped feta and peas. Return to the oven for 5 minutes.

Serve sprinkled with chopped coriander and lemon quarters.

NB. You can use rice, quinoa or other grains. For ease stir in microwaved rice.

JESSIE'S MASTELO

Slow cooked lamb with dill from the Greek island of Sifnos

Mastelo is the name of the clay pot that they cook this dish in on Sifnos, a Cycladean island famed for its food. Mastelo is popular at festivals and saints' day feasts, and the recipe varies from village to village. This is how I learned to make it. The quantities are approximate – precision is not necessary. I make it in my grandmother's crockery hotpot, and I cover the top with a double layer of greaseproof paper, tied tightly with string. Whatever you cover it with, it must be a good seal so no steam escapes. If you have a casserole dish with a lid, I would seal it with foil or greaseproof paper as well.

Ingredients:

- 1 shoulder of lamb (or you can mix leg and shoulder meat)
- 1 bottle of red wine
- 1 large bunch of dill (or you will need 2 packets of supermarket dill)
- sea salt.

I buy a whole shoulder of lamb and get the bone taken out. I cut it into 4 - 6 large pieces about the size of a clenched fist; once marinated, you need to be able to pack it tightly into the cooking dish with not much room left over.

I marinate the meat overnight in red wine (about half a bottle), a generous handful of chopped dill, and a very generous sprinkle of sea salt.

The recipe calls for a trivet of vine twigs in the bottom of the pot – I actually do this because I happen to have a vine in my garden, but you can also use some potato wedges – there just needs to be a small trivet in the base. Pack the meat in so it fits quite tightly, with an additional generous amount of chopped dill in between layers (but no more salt). Discard the marinade wine, but pour about 1.5 – 2 glasses of fresh wine over the top, and seal the pot (a lid alone is not enough). Put in the oven at 200ºC for an hour, then lower oven to 120º C for about 4 hours (depending how much meat you are cooking). It's not an exact science – when it's ready, the meat will just pull apart with 2 forks and be delicious and tender, but providing it's sealed properly, it's a very forgiving dish. There is no gravy with this dish. I pull the lamb apart and present it on a platter, garnished with wedges of lemon and rocket around the edges.

The Greeks would probably serve it with a tomato and onion salad, and maybe some sticky roast potatoes that they cook in olive oil, lemon juice, garlic and dried oregano with a dash of water that you replenish if they start sticking during the cooking.

DAISY'S SIMPLE ROAST CHICKEN

My feel good food is a simple roasted chicken! This is my feel good dish as this is the first thing my husband ever cooked for me when we first met and I instantly fell in love with him!

Method

Take the chicken out of its wrapping, place on a baking tray. Generously salt and oil the chicken skin (this will make for delicious, salty, crispy skin).

Cut up a few onions and place around the chicken. Put into the oven for 30-40 minutes, depending on the size of the chicken. Probe to make sure juices are running clear. Let the chicken rest for 10-15 minutes.

Once chicken is cooked, carve to your liking and keep the carcass!

Put that into a stock pot, along with some more onions, carrots, celery and cover with water. Reduce down to make stock. Once reduced, strain everything out with a sieve and incorporate your stock cube.

You can use any juice from your chicken earlier to add flavour. This should make a nice gravy to go with your roasted chicken.

Ingredients:

- any whole chicken
- onions
- salt
- oil
- chicken stock cube
- carrot
- celery

A guide for roasting your chicken:
Oven temperature 220C/200C fan/gas 7.

Roast for 45 minutes per kg, plus an extra 20 minutes to finish. Make sure the juices run clear when you put a skewer inside the leg joint.

LOUISE'S MARROW SURPRISE

This is my daughter's favourite dish. She asks me to make it when she visits and it is a real family favourite. It is very satisfying to make it for her knowing how much she loves it. This is a versatile dish, as a starter or main course.

Preparation time: 20 mins
Cooking time: until marrow is soft
Serves: variable

Ingredients:
- marrow, peeled, cubed and deseeded
- smoked bacon cut into small slices.
- tomatoes, tinned or fresh, chopped. (Care should be taken not to make it too wet , as marrow is very moist.)
- onion, sliced, a generous amount
- vegetable oil
- dried mixed herbs
- grated cheese

Method

For a main course use a greased, ovenproof dish, For a starter ramekins or similar can be used.

Lightly fry all of the ingredients, except the tomatoes, in the vegetable oil, transfer with a draining spoon to an ovenproof dish. Slightly brown the marrow on all sides and soften the onion.

Add chopped tomatoes straight from the tin. If using fresh, skin first. Stir in mixed herbs and seasoning. All ingredients should be evenly distributed. Sprinkle a generous amount of cheddar cheese on top.

Place in the middle of a medium oven, (approx. 160º C / 340º F / gas mark 3) until the marrow is really soft and the cheese is cooked. The time varies according to the size of the dish you are cooking.

Variations:
For vegetarians leave the bacon out. The marrow seeds can be left in. Chorizo sausage or any similar meat can be used instead of bacon. Courgettes make a good substitute for marrow.

To Serve:
As a main course serve on the table with a poached egg and crusty bread.
As an accompaniment, serve as a vegetable, with or without the cheese.
As a starter, put individual dishes on plates and serve with triangles of toast and a salad garnish.

SANJIDHA'S CHICKEN LAKSA

Enjoy! This is an easy recipe and always gets compliments

Serves: 4
Preparation time: 5 min,
Cooking time: 20 mins

Ingredients:

- chicken joints or pieces, or vegetarian alternative
- 4 spring onions
- 1 tbsp sesame oil
- 4 tbsp light soy sauce
- 1 tbsp fish sauce (optional)
- 2 garlic cloves
- 400ml light coconut milk
- 3cm root ginger
- 100ml chicken or vegetable stock
- 1 red chilli
- 4 nests of rice noodles
- 1 tsp turmeric
- 2 tbsp fresh coriander
- 2 tsp curry powder (med/hot)
- juice of ½ lime
- choice of veg (e.g. beansprouts, peppers, babycorn)

Method

In a saucepan, heat the sesame oil and fry the garlic, ginger, chilli, turmeric, and curry powder for 2-3 minutes.

Fry the chicken until cooked as per instructions on the pack.

Add the spring onions, vegetables, soy sauce, fish sauce, coconut milk, stock, and rice noodles.

Bring to the boil, then simmer for 5-10 minutes.

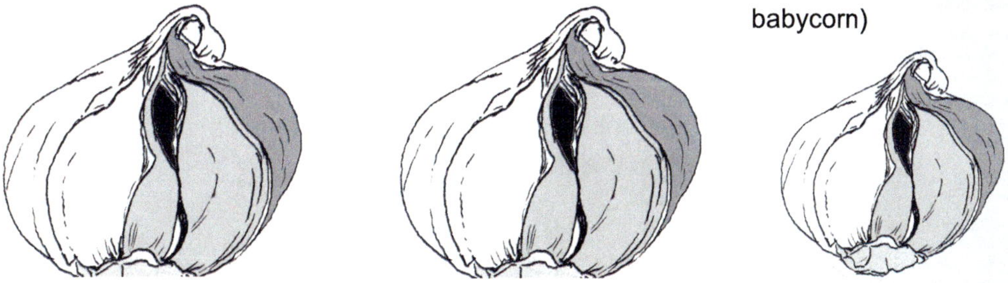

BEEF BOURGUIGNON FROM THE RED LION AT BRIDGE

Here is a recipe for a beef bourguignon. It is very easy to produce and very rewarding and comforting

Ingredients: serves 4-6

- 1.3kg braising steak
- 2 bay leaves
- 1 bunch fresh thyme
- 2 bottles cheap red wine
- 30g oil
- 2 large carrots
- 2 onions
- 27g plain flour
- 10g tomato purée
- 300g bacon lardons
- 150g silverskin onions
- 150g button mushrooms

Method

Cut 1.3kg of braising steak into large chunks. Marinate the beef in a large bowl with 2 bay leaves, a small bunch of fresh thyme, 2 bottles of cheap red wine and season with pepper. Cover and leave in the fridge overnight. On top of another bigger bowl, use a colander to strain the meat. Keep the wine.

Heat 15g of oil in a large frying pan, then brown the meat little by little, and transfer to a plate. When all the meat is browned, in the same frying pan pour a little wine to release any caramelised bits from the pan.

Heat 15g of oil in a large casserole. Cut 2 large carrots into big chunks, halve 150g of button mushrooms and roughly chop 2 onions, then fry them until they start to colour. Stir in 27g of plain flour for 1 min, then add 10g of tomato purée.

Add the beef and any juices, the wine from the frying pan and the rest of the wine that you used for marinating the beef. Season and bring to a simmer. Mix well and cover, then leave to cook on a low heat for 2 hours minimum. (Until the meat is really tender).

10 minutes before serving, in a frying pan cook 300g of bacon lardons and 150g of pickled silver skin onions. Once cooked, add to the beef bourguignon and serve. Can be served with classic mash potatoes, pasta or rice.

VIV'S IRAQI WHITE BEAN STEW

I love this recipe from Meera Sodha, published in the Guardian newspaper. It is easy to do and really warm and comforting. The lemon and coriander oil added at the end really gives an unusual twist and all in all it adds up to a mood lifting dish!

Method

Heat 3 tablespoons of oil in a large, heavy bottomed saucepan on a medium heat. Once hot, add the onions, a teaspoon of salt, the black pepper, cinnamon, allspice, cumin and coriander stalks, and cook, stirring occasionally, for 20 minutes, until soft and dark.

Keep an eye on it, as you don't want the onions and spices to catch.

When the mix is soft and sweet-smelling, add the tomatoes, beans and 200ml water, bring up to a boil, then simmer for 10 minutes.

In a bowl, mix two tablespoons of rapeseed oil, the coriander leaves, lemon zest and juice, and a quarter of teaspoon of salt.

To serve, divide the stew between four bowls and top with a generous spoonful of the coriander and lemon oil.

https://www.theguardian.com/food/2019/feb/02/meera-sodha-vegan-recipe-iraqi-white-bean-stew-fasoulia

Ingredients: serves 4.

- rapeseed oil for frying
- 2 brown onions, peeled and finely chopped
- salt
- ½ tsp ground black pepper
- ½ tsp ground cinnamon
- 1 tsp ground allspice
- ½ tsp ground cumin
- 50g fresh coriander, picked, stalks finely chopped
- 1 400g tin chopped tomatoes
- 2 400g tins cannellini beans, drained and rinsed
- 1 lemon, zested and juiced, to give about 3 tbsp lemon juice

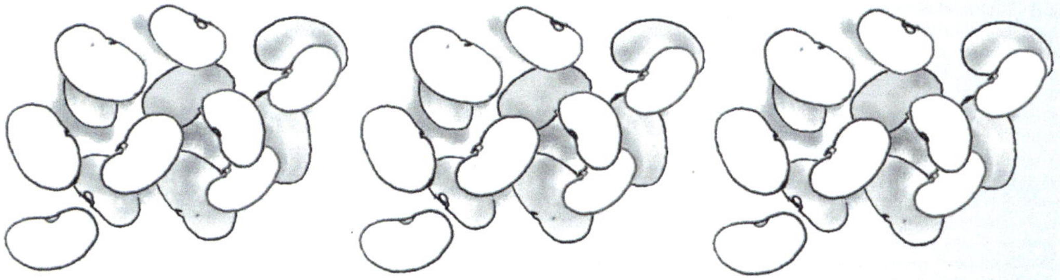

CHICKPEA & HARISSA STEW WITH PRAWNS

A quick mid-week dinner, that we enjoyed throughout lockdown, as it's cosy enough to be warming in the winter, but light enough to eat on a summer's eve.

Ingredients: serves 2

- 20 ml rapeseed oil
- 100g shallots
- 50 g chorizo (optional)
- 100 g peppers (red, yellow or a mix of the two for colour)
- 15g rose harissa paste
- 1 large tin of chickpeas (drained before use)
- 10 black olives (roughly - chopped)
- 5g capers (rinsed if stored in brine) finely chopped
- 150g raw peeled prawns
- 1 tbsp of plain yoghurt
- 2 cloves of garlic (minced or finely chopped)
- 75ml chicken stock (bouillon or oxo both work)
- fresh coriander and lemon juice to serve

Method

Peel and dice the shallots, dice the pepper and if using chorizo, slice it.

Heat the oil and sweat the vegetables (and chorizo if using) for approximately 2-3 minutes without allowing it to colour.

Stir in the garlic, for 1 minute, making sure it doesn't brown.

Add in the drained chickpeas and Rose Harissa Paste and cook for a further 2 minutes.

Add in the prawns and the chicken stock and simmer for 3-4 minutes until the prawns are cooked through.

Stir in the olives and capers and remove from the heat

Add the yoghurt and stir through while off the heat.

To serve, squeeze fresh lemon juice and sprinkle with chopped coriander leaves. While this works as a stew by itself, you can also add a pan fried fillet of fish (such as sea bass) over the top to complete.

EDIE'S GOAN PRAWN CURRY

This is a very easy meal. I don't work to a recipe but throw stuff in and hope for the best!

Method

Grind the spices together and add the vinegar to make a paste.

Chop and brown a large onion.

Add the masala and cook for a couple of minutes. Add the coconut milk and simmer for a couple of minutes more. Add the king prawns and simmer until cooked.

Optional

- handful of okra
- 10 curry leaves if available
- 3 pieces of Kokum* (Remove before serving)

Serve with plain rice or naan bread.

* Kokum is a fruit which is dried and used to add colour and a sweet / sour taste to curries.Tamarind can be used instead.

Ingredients:

For the masala:

- 2 Kashmiri chillies
- ¼ tspn cumin
- ¼ tsp peppercorns
- ½ tsp whole coriander seeds
- 1 tsp turmeric
- ½ inch ginger
- 2 cloves garlic
- 2 tbsp of malt vinegar
- 1 large onion
- ½ can coconut milk
- 250g king prawns

SLOW COOKER BEEF AND BROWN ALE STEW

I really enjoy hearty comfort food but I had found some recipes quite time consuming until I discovered the slow cooker - what a revelation! Now I had a way to cook that was easy, economical, and more importantly I didn't need to stay indoors to keep an eye on the pot! In the winter after spending time outdoors with friends and loved-ones, it makes me feel good to arrive home to the aroma of a warm and hearty stew ready to serve whenever we are ready. This is my favourite slow cooker recipe that epitomises hassle-free comfort food. It takes minimal preparation time, and the slow-cooked beef is just so soft and tender.

Ingredients: serves 4-6

- 4 rindless bacon rashers chopped
- 1 small onion chopped
- 45ml/3 tbs plain flour (or cornflour)
- 1kg lean stewing steak cut into chunks
- 30ml /2 tbs olive oil
- 500ml brown ale
- 1 tbs Dijon mustard
- 2 tbs honey
- 2 tbs dried mixed herbs
- salt and pepper

Method

Heat 1 tablespoon olive oil in a large saucepan and cook the bacon and chopped onion gently until lightly browned. Transfer to slow cooker.

In a bowl, season the flour with salt and pepper and toss the steak chunks in it, coating well.

Add the remaining olive oil to the pan and brown the meat quickly (you may need to do this in batches, transferring the meat to the slow cooker)

Add the ale to the saucepan, stirring gently while adding the mustard, honey and herbs. Bring to the boil before pouring over the meat in the slow cooker. Stir to mix the ingredients.

Cover and cook in the Slow Cooker on LOW setting for 6-9 hours, serve with fluffy mashed potatoes and vegetables.

BIRDIES LOCAL COD WITH COBNUT TOPPING

Courtesy of Birdies Restaurant, Harbour Street, Whitstable.
This recipe uses local fish and Kentish cobnuts. Birdies has been a favourite place to eat in Whitstable since 1993.

Method

Mix together the mascarpone cheese and the juice and grated rind of the lemon until it resembles a thick cream.

Lay the fish in an ovenproof dish. Spread the mascarpone mixture over the fish. Scatter the nuts over the top and pop into the oven for 20 min at gas mark 5, 120º C.

Serve with a spoonful of pesto trailed across the plate as decoration.

Simply delicious, as are most dishes from Birdies.

Ingredients: serves 4

- 4 pieces of cod (about 8 oz (225g) each)
- 1 small pot of mascarpone cheese
- 1 lemon
- salt and pepper
- 4 oz (110g) chopped, roasted cobnuts
- fresh red or green pesto

SANJIDA'S TERYAKI SALMON

To maintain heart health, we should all aim to eat one portion of oily fish each week - and luckily that includes salmon. This is an exciting recipe that will have you looking forward to consuming your weekly portion. Aristotle believed the heart was the source of our personality and there may be some truth to nurturing your physical health to improve your mental health. So why not start with the Teriyaki Salmon recipe below...

Preparation time: 10 mins
Cooking time: 40 mins
Serves: 2

Ingredients:

- 2 salmon fillets
- 1 tbsp sweet chilli sauce
- 1 tbsp honey, 1 tsp sesame oil
- 1 tbsp white wine vinegar
- 2 tbsp soy sauce
- 2 tsp finely grated ginger
- rice or noodles (optional)

For the pak choi:
- 2 large pak choi (250g)
- 2 tsp veg oil
- 2 tsp sesame oil
- 3 garlic cloves, grated
- 75ml fish or vegetable stock
- 2 tsp toasted sesame seeds

Method

Heat oven to 180ºC (160ºC fan) and put 2 salmon fillets in shallow baking dish.

Mix sweet chilli sauce, honey, sesame oil, rice wine vinegar, soy sauce and ginger in a small bowl and pour over salmon until covered.

Bake for 40 mins (or as per salmon instructions).

Cut a slice across the base of 2 large pak choi so the leaves separate.

Heat veg oil and sesame oil in a wok, add garlic cloves and stir fry.

Add the pak choi until leaves wilt. Pour over stock, tightly cover pan and cook for five mins.

Serve the pak choi in shallow bowls, top with salmon and spoon over juices. Scatter with toasted sesame seeds and serve with brown rice or noodles.

SWEET THINGS

CHEAT'S BREAD AND BUTTER PUDDING FROM PHOEBE'S CAFÉ

This dessert provides all you need for a comforting pudding in double-quick time.

Ingredients:

- 2 loaves of sliced fruit bread
- 2 cans of custard
- butter
- demerara sugar

Method

Spread butter onto the fruit loaf. Cut the slices into triangular shapes.

Place into a large oven-proof dish, point down, at an angle until the dish is full or all of the loaf has been used up.

Pour over the custard so that all of the bread is covered.

Sprinkle with brown sugar.

Bake at 180º C, 350º F or gas mark 4, for 35– 40 minutes.

SUMMER FRUIT FLAN

Fresh summer fruit served with ice cream or cream is a real summer treat. You can use strawberries, raspberries, black or red currants or any other soft fruit in season.

Method

Preheat the oven to 180°C (160°C fan), gas mark 4

Brush a 23cm / 9 inch flat tin with softened butter and line the bottom with non-stick baking paper.

Spread the fruit in the bottom of the tin. If the fruit is tart add a little sugar.

For the sponge:

Whisk the eggs and caster sugar together until the whisk leaves a thick trail across the surface, about 3 – 5 minutes.

Combine the almonds and flour and fold into the egg mixture keeping as much air in the mix as possible.

Spread the mixture on top of the fruit base and bake until the sponge has set, about 15 minutes or so.

Remove from the tin and place on your serving dish.

Preparation time:
10 -15 mins

Ingredients: Serves 4 to 6

- butter for greasing
- 450g soft fruit
- 2 eggs at room temperature
- 50g caster sugar
- 80g plain flour
- 50g ground almonds

THE PILOT INN, DUNGENESS
BANOFFEE PIE

This is a special treat to have after the Pilot's famous fish and chips - if you still have room!

Ingredients: Makes 10 large slices

- 450g digestive biscuits
- 300g butter melted
- 800g dulce de leche*
- 6 small bananas whole
- 600ml double cream
- 2 tbsp icing sugar
- 1 tbsp cocoa powder (to top)

* **Caramelised condensed milk** which can be bought in tins. **To make your own:** submerge a tin of sweetened, condensed milk in water and bring to the boil. Reduce to a simmer. Cook for 2-3 hours, the longer the darker the caramelization and vice versa. Keep an eye on the tins and make sure they are always under 2 - 3 inches of water. **Make sure the tin is completely cold before opening as the pressure builds up inside.**

Method

Crush the digestive biscuits by hand or in a food processor until you get fine crumbs. Mix the crushed biscuits with the melted butter. Pour the mixture into a loose bottomed tin. Push down to ensure the base is smooth.

Decant the caramel into a microwave proof bowl and melt until runny. Spoon it over the biscuit base and spread it out evenly using a knife.

Gently push the halved banana into the top of the caramel until the base is covered and refrigerate. Once set remove from the fridge and prepare the cream.

Whip the cream with the icing sugar until thick. Spoon the whipped cream on top of the bananas and dust the cocoa powder on top to decorate.

The Pilot Dungeness

Battery Road, Dungeness, Lydd-on-Sea, Kent, TN29 9NJ
01797 320314
info@thepilotdungeness.co.uk

THEA'S LEMON PUDDING

This recipe was scribbled out on a sheet of HM Stationary Office paper during a tea break in the Foreign Office back rooms in Burlington Gardens during the 1960s Satellite Conference. My fellow transcriber Armorel was the daughter of a chef who, in her words, 'took two years to learn about sauces, so by the time he got to puddings, he was pretty good.' This one is pretty good, and takes about 15 minutes to prepare.

Method

Separate the egg white and yolks, keeping both.

Put water in saucepan with sugar, grated rind and juice of 2 lemons, and bring to boil while you beat the separated egg whites to a snow.

Mix cornflour to a smooth runny paste with a little water.

Add this to the boiling lemon juice and beat all the time until it thickens.

Beat in the 2 egg yolks gradually.

Remove saucepan from heat and, when cooled a little, fold in beaten egg whites.

Ingredients:

- 2 lemons
- 2 eggs
- 2 tbsp cornflour
- 250ml water
- 225g caster sugar

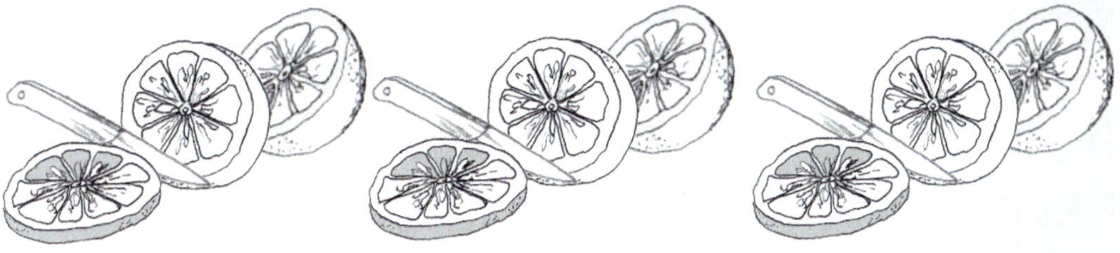

BOB'S SPECIAL APPLE DESSERT CAKE

This is a very old, well-used recipe! I don't use almond essence but sprinkle about ½ tsp cinnamon into the flour and some ground cloves over the apples. It freezes well.

Ingredients:

- 150g butter
- 2 large eggs
- 225g castor sugar
- 5ml almond essence
- 225g self-raising flour
- 1½ level tsp baking
- powder
- 675g cooking apples, before peeling
- icing sugar to dust

Method

Heat the oven to 190º C, 375º F, gas mark 5.

Grease well a 25cm, loose-bottomed cake tin.

Melt the butter in pan over a medium heat unril just runny and pour into a large bowl. Add the eggs, sugar and almond essence and beat well until mixed. Fold in the flour and baking powder.

Spread just under $^{2}/_{3}$ of the mixture into the cake tin.

Peel, core and slice the apples straight away and arrange on top of the mixture. Spread the remaining mixture over the apples. It is difficult to get this last bit of mixture smooth but don't worry as the blobs even out during cooking.

Bake for 1½ hours, but check the cake every ½ hour or so as sometimes it cooks in about an hour and may need covering with a "hat" of foil to stop it burning. It is done when the apple is tender when prodded with a skewer.

Loosen the sides of the cake with a knife and carefully push the cake out of the tin.

Dust very generously with icing sugar when slightly cooled and serve warm or cold with lots of lightly whipped or thick cream.

Keep covered in the fridge and eat within 4 days.

MARY'S LEMON SYLLABUB

This is an indulgent pudding but one to have occasionally to give yourself a treat. Try using 0% fat Greek yoghurt, half cream for a healthier dessert.

Method

Whip the cream and sugar together until soft peaks form.

Stir in the wine, most of the lemon zest and the juice.

Spoon into glasses or bowls, sprinkle with the remaining zest and serve with almond thins or berries.

Ingredients:

- 284ml tub whipping cream
- 50g caster sugar
- 50ml white wine
- zest and juice of half a lemon
- almond thins or berries, to serve

CHOCOLATE TART

With chocolate, syrup and cream, this is definitely an indulgence.

Preparation time: 20 mins + chilling

Cooking time: 20-25 mins

Serves: 6

Ingredients:

- 1 medium sized, ready cooked sweet pastry case
- 300ml double cream
- 25g golden syrup
- 50g soft brown sugar
- 350g chopped dark chocolate
- 75g unsalted butter
- 50ml whiskey or brandy

Method

Heat the cream until it boils. Take off the stove, add the syrup and sugar and stir until dissolved.

Add the chocolate and butter and melt gently.

Stir in the whiskey and brandy.

Let the mixture cool and then beat it until it emulsifies.

Pour into the pastry case and chill.

Serve with fresh berry fruit and more cream for a really luxurious dessert.

CHRISTMAS LOG

This is a star turn with the children. No oven is required to make this simple Christmas treat. Get creative with the decorations!

Method

Melt everything except the biscuits over a low heat. To avoid the chocolate over-heating, put the ingredients into a basin which just fits over a saucepan of boiling water. Stir until properly melted

Crush the biscuits into small pieces.

Pour the melted ingredients onto the biscuits and form the mixture into a log shape onto a plate. Melt the chocolate gently and "ice" the log. Scratch bark lines with a fork.

Add holly and tinsel and anything else Christmassy to make a table centrepiece.

Melting chocolate in a microwave:

Use a glass or ceramic bowl and melt the chocolate in short bursts, 20 or 30 seconds at a time.

Stir between heating.

Preparation time: approx. 20 mins

Cooking time: approx. 15 mins

Serves: 4 to 6

Ingredients:

- 250g digestive biscuits
- 110g margarine
- 1 tbsp sugar
- 2 tbsp cocoa
- 1 tbsp golden syrup
- vanilla essence

For the topping:

- 100g milk chocolate
- ½ tbsp milk

VANDA'S FLEXIBLE PANCAKES

This recipe was given to me by my sister, when she was still able to cook. This was one of her pleasures and she was able to cook pancakes when she couldn't manage more demanding recipes. Unlike most pancakes which are made in a frying pan, these are cooked in the oven.

You can serve these for breakfast, brunch or dessert and can even make a savoury version.

Ingredients:

- 15g butter
- 2 eggs, separated
- 80g plain flour
- 20g caster sugar
- 120ml milk

Method

Heat the oven to 220ºC, 200ºC Fan, Gas mark 7.

Melt the butter in a 20cm oven-proof dish.

Whisk the egg yolks with the caster sugar. Add the milk and flour and mix to a smooth paste.

Whisk the egg whites to stiff peaks and fold gradually into the mixture.

Pour into the dish and bake for about 15 minutes until firm.

You can add dried fruit into the mixture. Top with whatever you like; butter and maple syrup for breakfast, sliced soft fruit, fruit compote and, my favourite, marmalade warmed gently with a spoonful of water. Finish off with cream.

BAKING

GUY'S "MRS ROBIN'S FRUIT CAKE"

This fruit cake has helped along many Branch events, social and business. A Christmas regular!

The recipe is from Farmhouse Kitchen, published by Yorkshire Television in 1975. I have no idea who Mrs Robin is, as it doesn't say. It's just called her cake.

Ingredients:

- 4oz (110g) margarine
- 6oz (170g) granulated sugar
- 6oz (170g) sultanas
- 2oz (55g) chopped peel
- 8 oz (240ml) water
- 1 level tsp bicarbonate of soda
- 1 heaped tsp mixed spice
- 2 beaten eggs
- 4oz (110g) plain flour
- 4oz (110g) self-raising flour
- pinch of salt

Method

Place margarine, sugar, currants, sultanas, peel, water, bicarbonate of soda and mixed spice into a pan.

Bring to the boil and simmer for 1 minute.

Pour into a large mixing bowl.

Allow to cool.

Line a 7 inch (15cm) square or 8 inch (20cm) round cake tin with greased, greaseproof paper.

Add eggs, flours and salt to the cooled mixture, mix well, pour into tin.

Bake in the centre of the oven at gas mark 4, 350° F. for 1¼hours.

ANNIE'S ZUCCHINI NUT LOAF

Here's one of my favourite recipes which comes from a Canadian magazine 'Country Cooking 1983/84 during the year we lived in Guelph, Ontario. It's an easy loaf-tin cake I made just days after giving birth to our Canadian-born daughter on mid-summer's day in 1984 and is a trusted and well-tested cut-and-come-again moist cake! A brilliant stand-by as it keeps well in a tin or foil for a few days. Enjoy!

Method

In a large bowl stir together flour, salt, baking powder, baking soda, lemon peel, cinnamon and ginger – set aside.

In another bowl beat together eggs, sugar, oil and orange extract, if desired.

Add egg mixture to flour mixture along with zucchini and nuts; mix well.

Turn batter into a greased 9x5x3 inch loaf pan.

Bake in a 180º C / 350º F oven for 50-60 minutes or until wooden pick inserted in centre comes out clean.

Cool in pan for 10 minutes; remove from pan to wire rack.

Cool thoroughly. For a softer crust, wrap and store loaf overnight before slicing

Ingredients:

- 2 ½ cups (300g) all-purpose (plain) flour;
- ½ teaspoon salt
- 2 teaspoons baking powder
- 1 teaspoon baking soda
- 1 teaspoon finely shredded lemon peel
- ½ teaspoon ground cinnamon
- ¼ teaspoon ground ginger
- 2 beaten eggs
- 1 ¼ (125g) cups sugar
- ½ (120ml) cup cooking oil
- ¼ teaspoon orange extract (optional
- 2 cups (250g) finely shredded zucchini (courgette)
- 1 cup (150g) chopped walnuts (or mixed chopped nuts)

CHRISTINE'S AUBERGINE CHOCOLATE CAKE

Dairy-free, low fat and almost gluten-free, gooey cake. We first tasted an aubergine chocolate cake at our local health food café with our Saturday morning coffee. It became a seasonal treat and I have investigated a few recipes since the café closed. This one is the easiest, a combination of several.

Preparation time: 30 mins

Cooking time: approx. 40 minutes

Serves: about 8 slices

Ingredients:

- 225g or one medium aubergine
- 200g very dark cooking chocolate
- 3 medium eggs
- 150g runny honey
- 75g ground almonds
- 40g good cocoa powder
- 1.5tsp baking powder

Method

Grease a 20cm spring-form or cake tin with a loose bottom and line with greaseproof paper.

Wash the aubergine and prick all over with a sharp knife. Put into a microwaveable bowl, cover with cling film and microwave for about 3 mins. Leave to stand for 2 mins. If it is not very floppy, cook again for about 1 minute. Take the skin off with a sharp knife.

Add the other ingredients, except the baking powder, together in a large bowl. Beat until a bit fluffy.

While the aubergine is getting cool enough to handle, break the chocolate up small and add to the warm aubergine. The idea is to melt the chocolate until you can mix it in with the flesh to a smooth paste.

When the aubergine and chocolate is well mixed add it to the other ingredients and mix well. If the chocolate begins to set, put the mixture back into the microwave for 30 seconds to loosen it up.

Add the baking powder and mix well.

Pour the mixture into the lined cake tin.

Bake in the bottom of the oven for Fan oven 180º C / 350º F / Gas mark 4 about 40 minutes, or until a skewer pushed into the middle of the cake comes out clean.

Leave in the tin for 15 minutes before removing from the tin onto a cooling rack. Dust the top with icing sugar before serving.

To Serve: This cake is wonderful on its own but for a special occasion serve with whipped cream and berry fruits.

Note: If you haven't got a microwave cut the aubergine in half and score the flesh deeply. Put skin-side up on a greased tray and cook under a hot grill until the flesh is soft. Cover with cling film when done to make the skin easier to remove.

The chocolate can be melted in a bowl over a saucepan of hot water. Make sure you don't over-heat.

MATT'S BISCUITS

This is a super-quick recipe for a chocolate treat.

Method

Crush the biscuits up into small pieces.

Grease a shallow tray / cake dish (15cm or 6inches)

Heat the 100g butter/margarine, 25g cocoa powder, 75g golden syrup and 50g raisins in a pan.

Once all melted down, remove from the heat and add the crushed biscuits. Mix well.

Once all mixed together, spoon ingredients into the cake dish / tray. Press them into place.

Melt 100g plain chocolate – once melted, pour it over the biscuit mix and leave to cool in the fridge. Cut into squares once set.

Ingredients:

- 200g sweet biscuits (such as digestives without chocolate on them)
- 100g butter / margarine
- 25g cocoa powder
- 75g golden syrup
- 50g raisins
- 100g plain chocolate

ED'S BUTTERMILK TIN LOAF

I'm one of the many people who got into baking quite seriously during the Covid lockdown, having never baked anything before. My grandfather was a baker, so I like to think I'm carrying on the family tradition, even if it's skipped a generation! This loaf has become a firm favourite in our house. It's quite indulgent, as demonstrated by the amount of flour it requires! So perhaps not for your morning toast, but instead for a celebration, or with breakfast the day after a party. Could even be accompanied by a Bloody Mary (see my other submission!).

Ingredients:

- 670g strong white bread flour
- 17g fine sea salt
- 17g caster sugar
- 253ml warm water (around 40°C)
- 18g fresh yeast, or 7g fast action dried action yeast
- 35g unsalted butter, melted, plus extra for greasing the tin
- 170g buttermilk
- fine semolina for dusting
- water in a spray bottle

Method

Sift the flour into a large mixing bowl and stir in the sugar and salt. Pour the warm water into a jug and whisk in the fresh or dried yeast, then whisk in the melted butter, followed by the buttermilk.

Make a well in the flour, pour the liquid mixture into the well and bring everything together with a wooden spoon. Dust your worktop lightly with flour, then transfer the mixture to the worktop, using a dough scraper to get every last bit of dough from the bowl and spoon.

Dust your hands with flour and start to work the mix together.

As you are kneading the dough will start to form. Keep kneading for about 15 minutes or until the dough springs back nicely when you press your thumb into it.

Put the dough in a clean greased bowl, cover the bowl with clingfilm or a clean cloth and place in a warm spot for about one hour to prove.

The dough is ready when it has roughly doubled in size. Alternatively, put all the dry ingredients in the bowl of a stand mixer fitted with a dough hook and mix to combine.

Combine all the wet ingredients in a separate bowl, and add the wet ingredients to the dry ingredients in the mixer, and mix on a medium speed for about 10 minutes, then cover the bowl and leave to prove as before.

While the dough is proving, grease the inside of a 1.2 kg loaf tin lightly with butter, then put a little handful of flour in the tin and tip it around to make sure it covers every edge. Lightly knock any excess flour out.

Carefully transfer the risen dough to the worktop and gently knock it back.

Knead the dough lightly and tuck it into a nice shape that will fit snugly in the loaf tin, and place it in the tin.

Leave to prove again, covered loosely with clingfilm or clean cloth, for about 40 minutes in a warm spot, until the dough has doubled in size again.

Preheat your oven to 230° C.

Once the dough has risen again, use the water spray to coat the top of the dough with water, then dust the day with semolina using your hand. Finally, using a sieve, sprinkle it with a light coating of flour.

Put the tin loaf in the oven and bake for 10 minutes. After 10 minutes open the oven door and, working quickly, spray more water over the bread. Turn the temperature down to 180°C and bake for a further 20-25 minutes.

The bread is ready when you can remove it from the tin, tap the base and hear a slight hollow sound. If you think it needs a little longer, put it back in the tin and then back in the oven for a couple of minutes more at a time.

When ready, remove from the oven, turn the bread out of the tin onto a cooling rack and allow to cool for at least 30 minutes before slicing.

JUDITH'S SODA BREAD

Lovely recipe for great home-made bread without the effort; minutes to prep, and 40 to cook. I usually do half wholemeal and half rye flour, and add chia seeds to make it a superbread....

I found this recipe online during lockdown, and have not really bought bread

Preparation time: 10 mins

Cooking time: about 40 mins

Ingredients :

- 500gms wholemeal flour
- 2tsps sea salt
- 1tsp bicarbonate of soda
- 400 mls milk
- 1 lemon, juiced
- 2 tsps honey
- optional : 1tbsp finely chopped rosemary or handful of seeds

Method

Heat oven to 180º C / 350º F fan/gas 6.

Mix flour(s), salt, bicarb and any seeds or chopped herbs in a bowl.

Mix lemon juice and milk together to make buttermilk. Stir in the honey.

Pour milk mixture into flour mixture and stir with a knife until it is a sticky dough.

Tip out onto a floured surface or board, and shape into a ball.

Put ball onto a floured baking tray and pat into shape.

Make a deep cross in the top with a sharp knife.

Bake in the oven for 40 minutes.

Cool on a wire rack....or eat hot from oven!

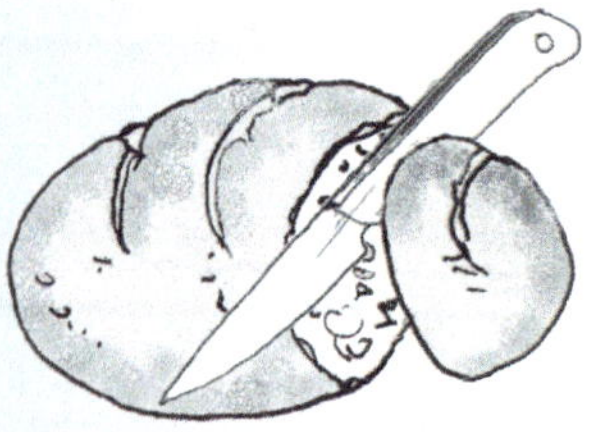

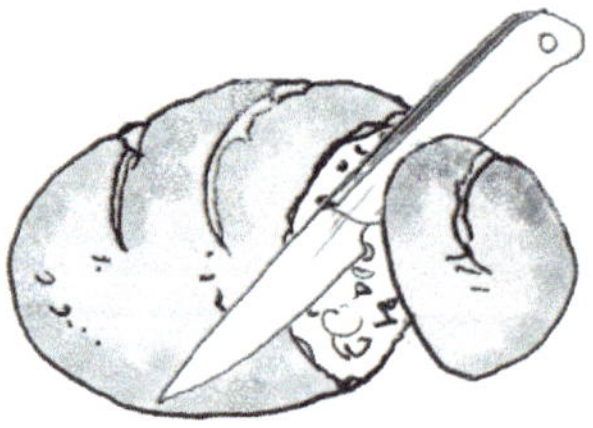

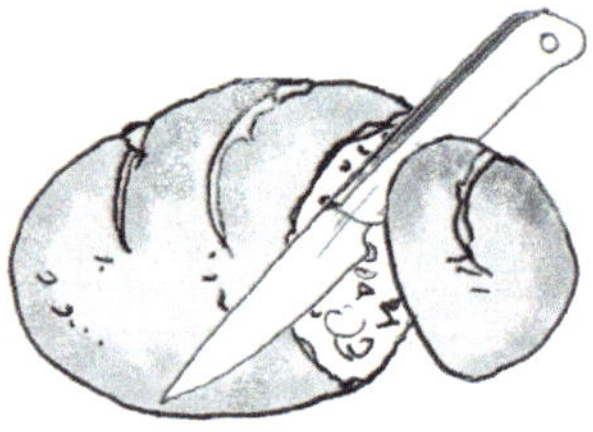

ENA'S EARL GREY TEA CAKE

I worked for Twinings tea for 17 years. Earl Grey was a frequent visitor to Twinings 216 Strand London. This is the Countess Grey recipe. I use two tea bags seeped in half a pint of freshly drawn water to soak the fruit.

Ingredients:

- 150g currants
- 150g sultanas
- 150g brown sugar
- finely grated rind of 2
- oranges
- 1/2 pint earl grey tea
- 275g self-raising flour
- 1 egg

Method

Put fruit, sugar and orange peel in a bowl, pour over Earl Grey tea. Cover and leave overnight.

Grease and line 8″ round cake tin, stir flour and egg into fruit mix.

Mix thoroughly and turn into cake tin.

Bake at 150° C / 300° F for 1 1/2 hrs.

Serve sliced with butter.

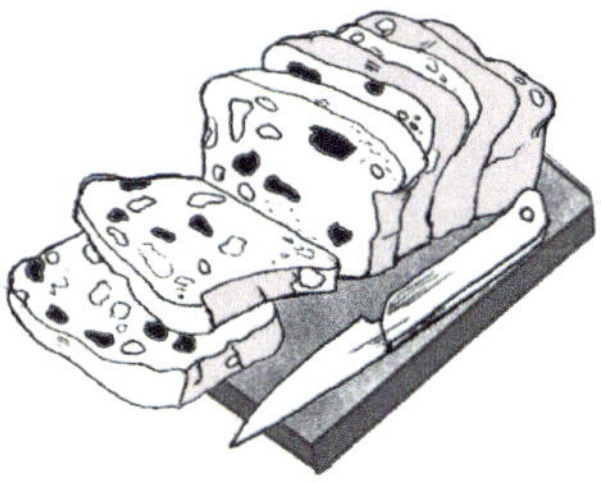

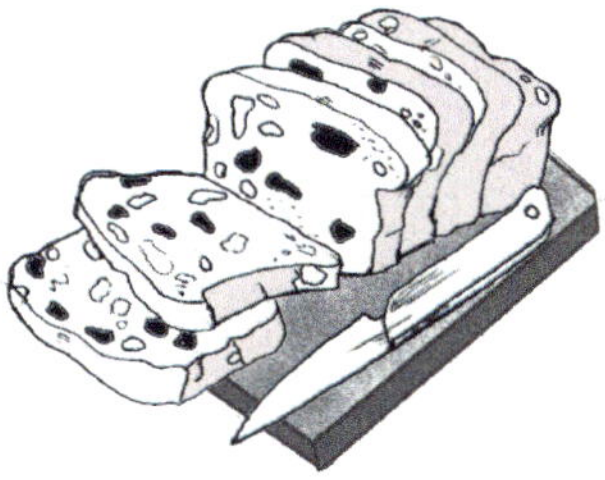

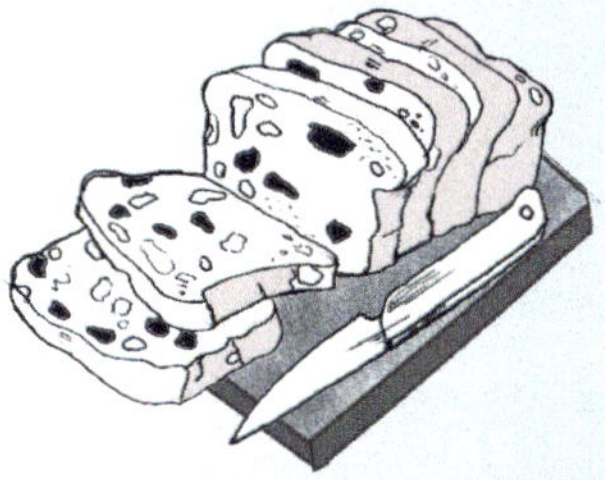

FEELGOOD FRUIT & NUT FLAPJACKS

These are quick and simple to make, store well and full of nuts and oats for an energy boost. It's a simple recipe with a bit of weighing and mixing with wooden spoon and has half the amount of sugar as our regular flapjacks we bake at Mama Feelgoods (as those have golden syrup and soft brown sugar instead of just the syrup!) You can also make this your own by switching the fruit and nuts for your favourites (or what you have in the cupboard) for example apricots and dates are a good swap for the sultanas. I have also baked this recipe with vegan butter as an alternative - found it a little crumblier but just as tasty.

Ingredients: Makes one tray bake .

- 250g oats
- 250g self raising flour
- 100g sultanas
- 250g golden syrup .
- 250g salted butter (block vegan butter works well too)
- 75g almonds - roughly chopped
- 75g hazelnuts - roughly chopped
- 25gm mixed Seeds - we use a salad mix that includes pumpkin & sunflower seeds

plus seeds to sprinkle on the top and chocolate of your choice to drizzle (optional)

Method

Line a 36cm x 26 cm (10x14") baking tray/roasting tin with baking parchment.

Mix all the dry ingredients together in a bowl.

Melt the butter and golden syrup and combine really well with dry ingredients.

Press into the tin lined with baking parchment and bake at 180° C for 15 - 20 mins or till golden.

Cool in the tray for 5 mins and cut whilst still in the baking tray into 24 squares before it sets.

Once cold you can drizzle with melted chocolate of your choice and sprinkle with a few extra seeds

Stores well for up to 6 weeks in an air tight container.

Tel: 01227 830830
Email: info@mamafeelgoods.com
Web: www.mamafeelgoods.com

OLIVE BREAD

This is a Greek recipe for a tasty bread to accompany your meal. The smell while it is cooking is as good as the loaves themselves.

Preparation time: 20mins + raising time
Cooking time: 30 – 45 mins
Makes: 2 loaves

Ingredients:

- 2 red onions
- 20ml / 2 tbs olive oil
- 225g pitted black olives
- 750 g strong, plain flour
- ½ tsp salt
- 7g dried yeast
- 3 tbsp chopped mint
- luke warm water

Method

Preheat the oven to 220º C, 425º F.

Thinly slice the onions and fry in the olive oil until soft. Roughly chop the olives.

Put the flour, salt, yeast and mint in a large bowl together with the fried onions and olives and mix.

Pour in 475ml lukewarm water. Mix to a dough. If the mixture feels dry add a little more water.

Turn out onto a floured surface and with floured hands knead for about 10 minutes. Put into a clean bowl, cover with lightly oiled cling film and leave in a warm place until doubled in size. Depending on how warm it is, this will take about an hour.

Turn the dough onto a floured surface and cut in two. Pat these into rounds (be rough with the dough!) and put onto greased baking sheets. Cover loosely with oiled cling film and leave until doubled in size.

Remove the clingfilm and use a sharp knife to slash the tops of the loaves.

Bake for about 40 mins. Check that they are done by tapping the bottom of the loaves which should sound hollow.

Transfer to a wire rack to cool.

OMA SAMSON'S DATE AND WALNUT LOAF.

Family recipes are very precious. This one, safely held in a handwritten notebook, is one of our family traditions.

Ingredients:

- 340g plain flour
- 120g caster sugar
- 1 level teaspoon salt
- 50g chopped walnuts
- 225g chopped stoned dates
- 2 tablespoons corn or sunflower oil.
- 1 egg
- 2 level teaspoons bicarbonate of soda
- 250ml boiling water

Method

Grease a 2lb loaf tin.

Sift flour, sugar, salt into a mixing bowl.

Add the walnuts and dates.

Whisk together the corn oil and egg and add them to the dry ingredients.

Dissolve the bicarbonate of soda in the boiling water and stir into the dry ingredients when cooler.

Beat well to form a slack mix and pour into the prepared tin.

Bake 180° C, 350° F degrees gas mark 4, for 1 hour 15 minutes.

Serve sliced with butter.

CINNAMON BUNS

This recipe was sent to us by the friend of a friend of a friend and had been translated from Latvian somewhere along the way. These wonderful, aromatic buns have become a tangible link in the way in which sharing recipes and food can make precious connections to people and places.

Method

Dough preparation:
Put everything in the mixing bowl and knead a sticky, shiny dough, put it in the bowl and leave it to warm for about 40 minutes. (I normally start from mixing warm milk with sugar, salt and yeast, then mix in butter, eggs and finally sifted flour).

Filling preparation:
Using a mixer, beat the softened (I normally use melted as it's easier to spread) butter with brown sugar and cinnamon (and cocoa if used) until smooth.

Forming muffins:
Roll out the risen dough into a square, apply filling evenly, and fold the edges inward (please see diagrams below).

Cut into 12 strips and cut each strip into 3 slits. Braid the dough, twist the ends, place in cupcake moulds and bake at 180º C 160º C fan for around 30 minutes.Check the buns after 20 mins and assess the final cooking time.

Ingredients:

For the dough:

- 300g of flour
- 7g dry yeast (1 pouch)
- 100g milk (warm)
- 1 egg
- 100g butter (melted but not hot)
- 30g sugar
- a pinch of salt

For the filling:

- 75g soft butter (I normally use melted)
- 125g brown sugar
- 1 tsp cinnamon
- 2 tsp cocoa (optional for chocolaty taste)

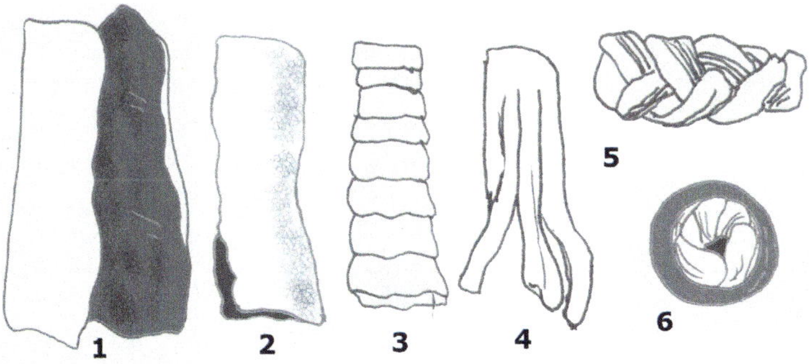

BOB'S SOURDOUGH BREAD

ALL SORROWS ARE LESS WITH BREAD. CERVANTES

A sourdough starter is a culture of natural yeasts grown in your bread flour. It takes a while to make but a good starter can last for years, with attention. Part of the starter is used each time to make a loaf. There are various ways to make a starter. A comprehensive description can be found at https://en.wikipedia.org/wiki/Sourdough#Starter

Ingredients:

Big Loaf:
- 200g of starter
- 650g of bread flour
- 400ml of lukewarm water
- 12g salt

Medium Loaf:
- 140g of starter
- 455g of bread flour
- 280ml of lukewarm water
- 8g of salt

Small Loaf:
- 100g of starter
- 325g of bread flour
- 200ml of lukewarm water
- 6g of salt

Method

Starter: Discard all but 100g of your starter. Mix in 100g of bread flour and 100ml of lukewarm water. Mix carefully. The consistency should be a thick paste. Leave at room temperature loosely covered. You can feed your starter with white, wholemeal or rye flour. Try to avoid keeping your starter in plastic. A glass jar is ideal. I use an 850ml Weck jar. (Any large jar will do.)

It can be helpful to mark the level of the starter after feeding. You can write straight on the glass with a sharpie or put an elastic band around the jar.

If you are going to bake that day allow the starter approx 6 to 8 hours to rise a little. It should roughly double. The best time to use your starter is just after it has peaked and started to fall. You can usually tell it is falling by streaks on the side of the jar. You can check if it is ready by dropping a teaspoonful in water. It will float if ready.

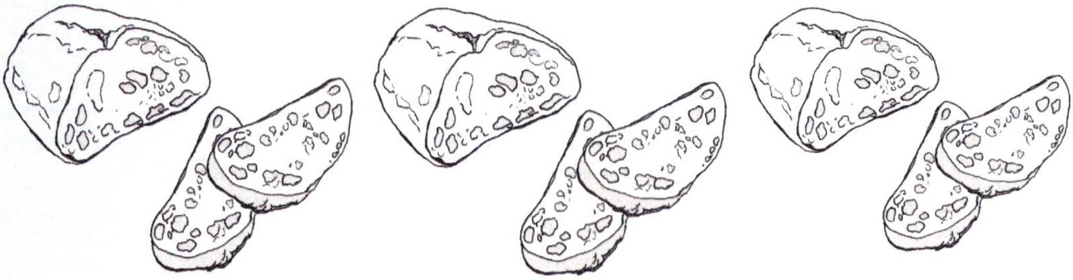

If you are not planning to bake regularly keep your starter in the fridge tightly covered. Feed as above once a week allowing the starter a bit of time out of the fridge after feeding to wake up before popping it back in the fridge. You will occasionally have some discard starter left after a feeding. This can be used in a variety of recipes or thrown away or given to a friend!

Day One of Baking Bread

Approx 10am - Take your starter out of the fridge and feed it as above.
Approx 6pm - in a bowl mix the following. Stir well. The mixture will be a bit lumpy and sticky. That is fine. Cover with a tea towel and leave for 45minutes.
Approx 7pm - stretch and fold your dough in the bowl. There is a video on YouTube called 'Sourdough Folding Method ' by a channel called 'Cup of Flour' which explains this technique.
Approx 8pm - as above
Approx 9pm - as above
Approx 10pm - pull your dough out of the bowl and shape on a floured surface. There are loads of dough shaping videos on Youtube. Place in a clean oiled bowl, cover with a tea towel and leave overnight in the fridge.

Day Two of Baking Bread

When you get up - turn on the oven as hot as it will go. 220º C approx
If you have a Dutch oven (cast iron casserole dish with a lid) or a heavy ceramic casserole dish with a lid put this into the oven to heat up too. This should go in when the oven is first turned on to avoid cracking the enamel. The purpose of the Dutch oven is to seal in the moisture whilst the bread is baking as this helps it to rise and form a crunchy crust.
Take your bowl of dough out of the fridge. Is the top sticky? If so, sprinkle a little flour on top. Place the palm of your hand onto the top of the dough and flip the bowl so you end up with the dough resting on your hand. Slip this straight into the hot Dutch oven or onto a floured baking sheet.
You can flour and score the bread if you like. I use a tomato knife to do this.
Put the lid on the dutch oven if using and put the bread into the oven for 30 to 35 minutes covered and approx 10 minutes uncovered. The crust should be a warm strong brown in colour.
You should have starter left over which you can feed and use again.

ALMOND TORTE WITH LEMON SYRUP

When, some years ago, I discovered I was gluten/dairy intolerant, I thought the days of enjoying cake were over. But then I found this one, which even gluten/dairy-loving folk enjoy too. These days, the free-from sections in supermarkets offer more choice for the likes of me, but this moist lemony cake remains a favourite. It also makes a great summertime pudding served with strawberries/raspberries, and yoghurt/cream/ice-cream (or dairy-free alternatives!)

Ingredients:

For the cake:

- 300g ground almonds
- 4 medium eggs, separated
- 250g caster sugar
- grated zest of 1 unwaxed lemon and 1 tbsp juice
- 1 tsp ground cinnamon

For the syrup:

- 25g caster sugar
- pared zest and juice of 1 unwaxed lemon
- icing sugar – to dust to serve

Method

Preheat oven to 175ºC. Grease a 20cm round loose-bottomed cake tin and line with baking parchment.

Whisk together the egg yolks, sugar, lemon zest and juice until it becomes thick, pale and creamy.

Mix together almonds and cinnamon in a large bowl, and then add the egg yolk cream – it will be quite dry and stiff.

Whisk the egg whites until they form stiff peaks. Using a metal spoon, lightly fold 2 table spoons of egg white into the almond mixture to loosen it slightly, then gently fold in the rest.

Pour the mixture into the tin and bake for approx. 45 mins or until a skewer comes out clean. (I usually check after 30 mins – if the top is colouring too much, cover the surface with a piece of foil). Leave to cool in the tin. While the cake is cooling, make the syrup. Put the pared zest, lemon juice and sugar plus 1 tablespoon water in a small pan. Heat gently until sugar has dissolved.

Using a skewer, make deep holes all over the surface of the cake. Spoon the syrup over the cake.

Dust the top with icing sugar to serve.

AND...

ED'S BLOODY GOOD BLOODY MARY

The spice mix for this drink is best left in the fridge to mature for a week or so before use. It'll keep for around a month, so it's a good thing to have "on standby" over the festive season, or when you know you'll be celebrating a special occasion. The spice mix need not be terribly accurate in terms of measuring, and things only need roughly chopping.

Ingredients: for one

a measure of vodka

Spice mix:

- 290ml Worcestershire Sauce
- 1 lemon, washed and chopped
- 2 garlic cloves, chopped
- A small bunch of coriander, washed and chopped
- 1 fresh red chilli, washed and chopped
- A thumb sized piece of fresh ginger, washed and chopped
- 1 lemongrass stalk, chopped
- 1 tsp of celery salt
- Freshly ground pepper

Method

Put 50ml good quality vodka into a container of your choice.

Add 30ml spice mix

Add ice if you fancy it

Mix in 125ml chilled tomato juice

A small stick of celery and a slice of lemon make a good garnish.

Enjoy!

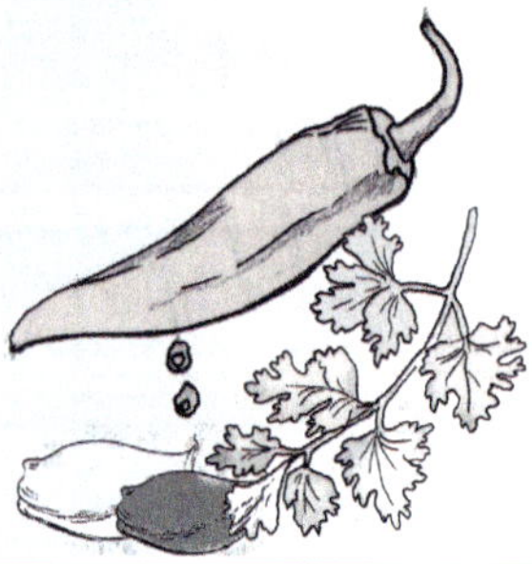
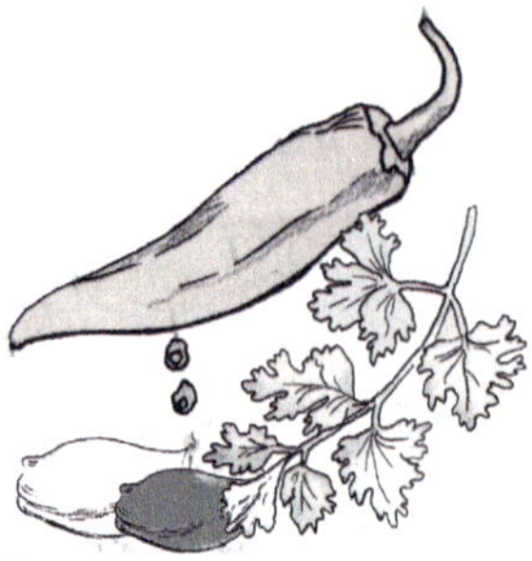
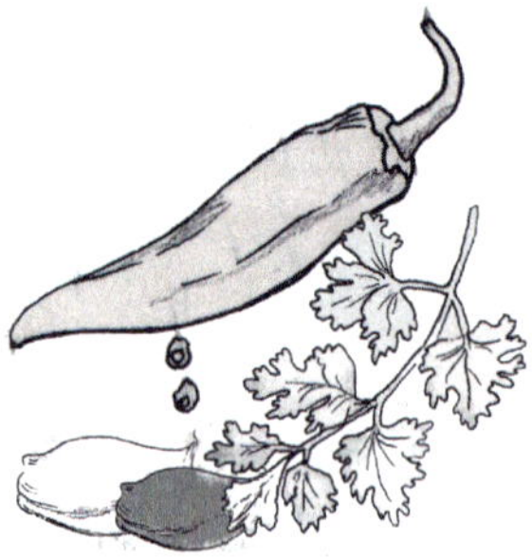

EDIE'S CHAI MASALA

This is a warming and comforting cup of chai.

Method

Dry roast on a low flame and set aside the cardamom, cloves, pepper, cinnamon and fennel.

Dry roast the dried ginger, tulsie and nutmeg.

Grind all the spices when cool in a coffee grinder and store in airtight container

Boil 2 cups of water, add 2-4 teaspoons of tea leaves and 1/2 teaspoon of your Chai Masala.

Bring to boil

Add 1 cup of milk and sugar to taste.

Ingredients:

- 20g cardamom seeds
- 10g cloves
- 10g pepper
- 4g cinnamon
- 5g fennel
- 30g dried ginger
- 6 tulsie leaves*
- 1/2 nutmeg
- 2–4 tsp tea leaves
- 1 cup milk
- 1–2 tsp sugar to taste

*Tulsie is sometimes called Holy Basil. Italian or Thai basil can be used instead.

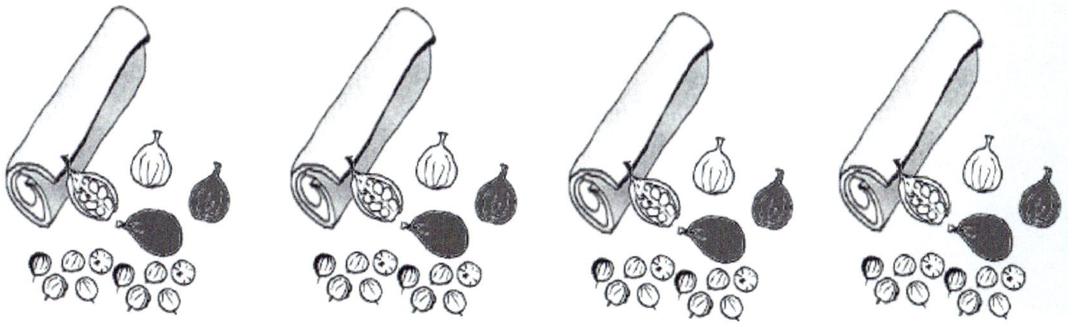

HELENA'S LEMON CURE

My recipe which is more of a healing potion than a meal recipe. It is excellent o0ir flu and colds but you don't need an excuse to enjoy its restorative properties.

Ingredients:

-1 lemon
- honey, runny or set, any will do but the Multifloral Manuka honey is very healthy. It is available in the cheaper stores at a better price!
-1 clove garlic, or 2 depending on taste
- small piece of fresh peeled ginger, sugar cube size.

Method

Thinly slice half a washed lemon and put into heat proof glass or a mug. Juice the other half of lemon and add the juice to the sliced lemon.

Add 2 or 3 teaspoons of honey, leave spoon in the glass.

Crush the garlic and add it to the glass.

Finely chop the peeled fresh ginger and add it to the glass.

Pour on boiling water and stir until the honey has all dissolved in the water.

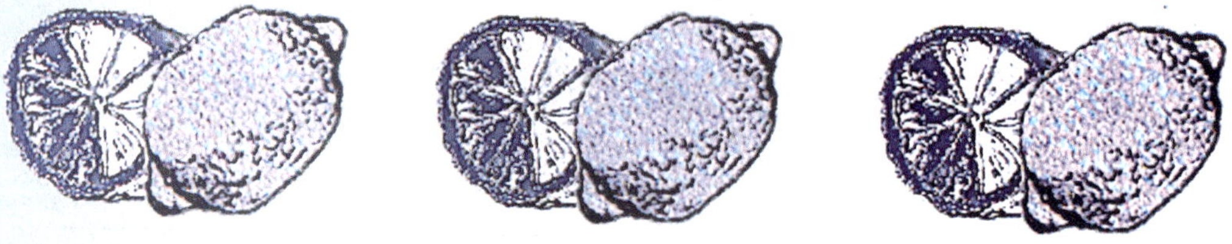

KATE'S HEDGEROW JAM

There are few things more reassuring than a cupboard full of homemade jam. The satisfaction increases if the fruit has been gathered on a walk through the autumn countryside. This recipe came from a friend who spent a long time foraging for delicious (and sometimes not so delicious) free food.

Ingredients:

-any combination of blackberries, elderberries, damsons, crab apples etc.
-hazelnuts
-sugar.

Method

Weigh and cook the fruit until it is soft. If you don't like pips keep the blackberries and elderberries separate and strain through a jelly bag or muslin cloth when cooked.

Measure the strained pulp.Add 1Kg sugar to each Kg fruit or litre of pulp.

Boil together until the setting point is reached, 105º C. If you don't have a jam thermometer drop a small amount onto a cold saucer. If it cools quickly so that a spoon makes a clean line through the jam it is probably done.

Add halved or whole hazelnuts and stir through.

Leave to stand for a few minutes before potting into sterilised jars. Cover with a waxed disc and cellophane lids.

To sterilise the jars, make sure they are very clean. Place on a tea towel on a baking tray and heat in the oven to about 140º C. You can allow then to cool a little before filling.

MRS NAROZNIK'S PICKLED MUSHROOMS

When I was a student in London I was very hard-up and anything which boosted my budget was very welcome. My landlady gave me quantities of pickled mushrooms, the recipe for which I think originated in Poland. I hated them at first but ate them out of necessity and soon grew to quite like them. My friends were quite keen, treating them like an exotic novelty. I have only once made them myself in the spirit of recreating my student days. I still didn't really like them.

Ingredients:

- 250g button mushrooms
- 500ml white malt vinegar
- 2 blades mace
- 4 peppercorns, lightly crushed
- 1 tsp ground ginger or a piece of fresh ginger as big as a thumbnail
- 2 peeled cloves of garlic
- ½ onion, finely chopped
- 1 tsp salt

Method

Wash and dry the mushrooms, trim the stalks and cut any large ones in half.

Put into a saucepan and just cover with the vinegar.

Stir in the rest of the ingredients and bring to the boil.

Cover and simmer gently for 10 – 15 minutes.

Meanwhile, sterilise clean jars and vinegar-proof lids by heating in the oven to 160º C for 15 minutes.

Remove the mushrooms with a straining spoon and fill the jars tightly.

Strain over enough hot vinegar to cover and seal immediately.

Leave for at least two weeks before using.

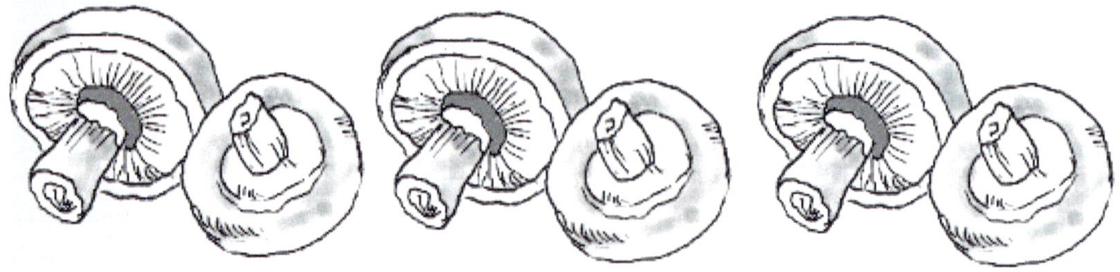

GREEN TOMATO MARMALADE

One thing we can usually be sure of in the garden is that many of the tomatoes will not ripen at the end of the season. This recipe is a marvellous way of making sure nothing goes to waste. Friends are initially sceptical at making marmalade out of tomatoes but they usually come round when they try it.

Ingredients:

- 5 lemons
- water
- 1 kg green tomatoes
- 1.8 kg sugar

Method

Wash the lemons, halve them and squeeze out the juice. Remove the remaining flesh and put it, and the pips, into a muslin cloth or jelly bag. Strip away the pith, cut the peel into thin strips and put into a pan. Add 400 ml water and simmer for 20 mins.

Meanwhile, cut the tomatoes into quarters, remove the core and pips and tie into the jelly bag with the lemon flesh and pips.

Shred the tomato flesh and place into a preserving pan with the lemon juice made up to 1.8 l with water. Add the softened lemon peel, plus the water. Simmer together until tender - about 40 mins.

Add the sugar, stirring all the time and boil briskly until the setting point is reached. This can take ages but if it works well the tomato flesh will taste a little like candied peel.

When ready, put into sterilised jars and cover in the normal way. See "Hedgerow Jam" for how to sterilise the jars.

ACKNOWLEDGMENTS

Thank you to the following cafés and restaurants who have generously shared their recipes:

The Folkestone Wine Company: 5 Church St, Folkestone, Kent, CT20 1SE
Tel: 01303-249952
https://folkestonewine.com/

Phoebe's Coffee House and Sandwich Bar: Ivy Lane, Canterbury, CT1 1TU
Tel: 01227 500451

Mama Feelgoods: Bekesbourne, Canterbury, Tel: 01227 830830
www.mamafeelgoods.com

The Coffee Corner: 51 -52 St Dunstans St., Canterbury CT2 8BS

The Pilot: Battery Rd, Lydd-on-Sea, Romney Marsh TN29 9NJ
Tel: 01797 320314
thepilotdungenesas.co.uk

The Red Lion Inn: 5 High Street, Bridge, Canterbury CT4 5LB
Tel: 01227832213
www.redlionbridge.co.uk/

Birdies Restaurant: 41 Harbour Street, Whitstable, CT5 1AH,
Tel: 01227 265337
https://www.birdiesrestaurant.co.uk/

Gwesty Cymru: 19 Marine Terrace, Aberystwyth, Ceredigion. SY23 2AZ
Tel: 01970 612252
https://gwestycymru.com/

THANK YOU...

Volunteers, past and present, contributed to this book. A special thanks goes to Geoff and Mandy, who created the first Canterbury and District Cookery Book some years ago which gave us the idea of an updated version.

Thanks too to the volunteers who helped with proof-reading, editing and general dogsbody tasks: Martin, Thea, Beth, Peter, Leo, Jessica, Kara and Bess.

Tom, Leo and the Trustees got behind the project from the start and Olivia helped with finances.

The Editorial and creation team were Jan, Ena, Phoebe, Sanjida, Jessie, Jessica and Christine.

Illustrations are by Christine

Apologies to anyone we have missed. This was a whole branch venture and many volunteers gave their encouragement and support.

Thank you all!

ABOUT SAMARITANS

Every 10 seconds, Samaritans responds to a call for help. We're here, day or night, for anyone who's struggling to cope, who needs someone to listen without judgement or pressure.

Samaritans is not only for the moment of crisis, we're taking action to prevent the crisis. We give people ways to cope and the skills to be there for others. And we encourage, promote and celebrate those moments of connection between people that can save lives.

We offer listening and support to people and communities in times of need. In prisons, schools, hospitals and on the rail network, Samaritans are working with people who are going through a difficult time and training others to do the same.

Every life lost to suicide is a tragedy, and Samaritans' vision is that fewer people die by suicide. In 2021, around 22,000 people volunteered their time for Samaritans.

We make sure people have somewhere to turn, and support when they need it most. We work with communities to let people know we're here for them and we campaign to make suicide prevention a priority. We listen without judgement and give people the time and space to come to their own decisions.

To find out more, visit www.samaritans.org

To contact our listening service call 116123.
This 24-hour telephone line is free.
Email us on jo@samaritans.org
For other ways to access our service go to www.samaritans.org

INDEX

INDEX, CONTINUED

Printed in Great Britain
by Amazon

13317761R00045